QUINTET

themes & variations

*For Emily
with love,
from
Jean*

QUINTET

themes & variations

Jean Mallinson   Pam Galloway   Eileen Kernaghan
Sue Nevill   Clélie Rich

Ekstasis  Editions

Canadian Cataloguing in Publication Data

Main entry under title:
    Quintet

    Poems
    ISBN 1-896860-25-7

    1. Canadian poetry (English)--Women authors.
2. Canadian poetry (English)--20th century. I. Title.
PS82838.R694H57   1998   C811'.54   C98-910835-7
PR9199.3.T68H57   1998

Cover Art: Noreen Tomlinson
Author Photo: Stewart Fairley

Acknowledgement:
Thanks, from the authors of *Quintet: Themes & Variations*, to the periodicals and publications in which some of these poems first appeared: *The Amethyst Review, The Antigonish Review, Black Lotus, Contemporary Verse 2, Dandelion, The Fiddlehead, Fireweed, In All Her Rooms* (Reference West), *Motherwork, The Malahat Review, The Muse Journal, The Mythic Circle, The New Quarterly, Prairie Journal of Canadian Literature, PRISM International, Tesseracts 5, Tesseracts 6, TickleAce, Wascana Review.*

Published in 1998 by:
Ekstasis Editions Canada Ltd
Box 8474, Main Postal Outlet
Victoria, B.C., V8W 3S1

Ekstasis Editions
Box 571
Banff, Alberta T0L 0C0

THE CANADA COUNCIL | LE CONSEIL DES ARTS
FOR THE ARTS | DU CANADA
SINCE 1957 | DEPUIS 1957

Quintet: Themes & Variations has been published with the assistance of grants from the Canada Council and the Cultural Services Branch of British Columbia.

Female Complaint	Eileen Kernaghan	62
If Only	Jean Mallinson	63

Postcards

News From ...	Jean Mallinson	67
laughing down the avenues	Clélie Rich	68
Ice Songs	Eileen Kernaghan	69
always toward mountains	Sue Nevill	70
Parallel lines	Pam Galloway	71

Unexpected Gardens

sage hills	Sue Nevill	75
the roses in the carpet	Clélie Rich	76
Unexpected Gardens	Pam Galloway	77
fractal image	Eileen Kernaghan	78
A Dispraise of Mushrooms	Jean Mallinson	79

Secret Animals

The Temperamental Garden——Page 31	Sue Nevill	83
Butterflies	Pam Galloway	84
through the window of the garden shed	Eileen Kernaghan	85
tonight is an angry wind	Clélie Rich	86
Breath begins	Jean Mallinson	87

At the Level of Water

lunary	Clélie Rich	91
Flux	Pam Galloway	92
Water is verbs	Jean Mallinson	93
Transitive	Sue Nevill	94
my being rises, goes to my nature	Eileen Kernaghan	95

Thoughts of the Sky

Ascension	Eileen Kernaghan	99
cante	Clélie Rich	100
Running for Paradise	Sue Nevill	101
Attributes of Angels	Jean Mallinson	102
November Lights	Pam Galloway	103

The Other Side of Passion

The artist's wife	Pam Galloway	107
In the garden of the sixth empress	Eileen Kernaghan	108
one floor below	Sue Nevill	109
Seeing	Jean Mallinson	110
affidavit	Clélie Rich	111

Broken Syllables

Breakdown	Pam Galloway	115
the weight of breathing	Clélie Rich	116
plain chant	Sue Nevill	117
Speech Acts	Jean Mallinson	118
broken syllables	Eileen Kernaghan	119

Contents

eyes so wide and filled with leaves   *Sue Nevill*   8

Memory Lies in the Body

Caught Soul	*Pam Galloway*	11
in the body	*Sue Nevill*	12
the ghost of wine	*Clélie Rich*	13
questionnaire	*Eileen Kernaghan*	14
Like Mother	*Jean Mallinson*	15

Forgotten Arts

I have forgotten the arts of love	*Jean Mallinson*	19
Open stock	*Sue Nevill*	20
Queen of Red Clay	*Pam Galloway*	21
juego de palmas	*Clélie Rich*	22
The Language of Cigarettes	*Eileen Kernaghan*	23

Old Words

Power Shifts	*Jean Mallinson*	27
The Other Side of Life	*Eileen Kernaghan*	28
Break	*Pam Galloway*	29
NB: Make glasses in order to see moon large.	*Sue Nevill*	30
shadow of the birdfeeder	*Clélie Rich*	31

Living Ghosts

the phantom captain	*Clélie Rich*	35
November 11th, 1994	*Eileen Kernaghan*	36
In the grain	*Pam Galloway*	37
step	*Sue Nevill*	38
All those years	*Jean Mallinson*	40

Strings

Kandinsky's Colours	*Eileen Kernaghan*	43
long term	*Clélie Rich*	44
Spinning tops, chalk and string	*Pam Galloway*	45
Labyrinth	*Jean Mallinson*	46
moon marks	*Sue Nevill*	47

In the Thick

rough terrain	*Eileen Kernaghan*	51
past the bone	*Clélie Rich*	52
The Jewish Bride	*Sue Nevill*	53
touching the past	*Pam Galloway*	54
Through Thick and Thin	*Jean Mallinson*	55

Going to Extremes

parosmia	*Clélie Rich*	59
Blood lines	*Sue Nevill*	60
Howling	*Pam Galloway*	61

Preface

Quintet: Themes & Variations, the work of five women writing in concert, originated as an exploration of the poetic possibilities of shared themes. This collaborative venture evolved into a series of well-received public readings whose structure has led, in turn, to this book.

eyes so wide and filled with leaves

how confident we were at the beginning of the story
in the strength of breadcrumbs and the friendliness
of birds in our certainty of which way moss points

halfway along our journey now at the mark past which
survival is intentional these crossed roads force us
to look down and claim our feet

are we the passionate runaways or the confiding
toddlers abandoned in a green maze by our wicked
dreams we cannot remember

was it doves who followed us feeding on the fragments
of ourselves we threw away or vultures   how can we
tell the wolf from the family dog our eyes so wide now
and filled with leaves and what is this footprint labyrinth
this encirclement of past impressions still trembling from
the hoarse breath of someone running

Sue Nevill

Memory Lies in the Body

Caught Soul

Canaries' brains are so very small
they remember little, restart their lives
every two minutes,
the scientist says.

Another says memory lies
in each cell, something tangible
like a drop of water or blood.

It's not in the eyes then,
dry reflection of a caught soul
but in each tilt of the head
toward daylight, each brush with steel.
The spirit drowns in recollections
of an open sky.

Pam Galloway

in the body

beauty lies in the body

beauty lies to the new body saying

> *i am all you need and will be with you*
> *forever*

and there is almost truth to this
like all good lies   beauty
makes deep memories

we claim we always sought for
beauty without good bones without
the shining hair and muscled spine
beauty detectable in streams of vivid words
and laughter   remembering this aloud too clearly
too often for belief

mind lies
the body does not lie   the proof
is in the ageless summer turning of heads

memories of beauty   ours and theirs
lie in the body like untriggered mines
exploding in boardrooms   in another's arms
and memory lies to the body
its always-smooth palms stroking
always faultless skin

Sue Nevill

the ghost of wine

decades since his death and still
her body misses him
she lights candles
uncorks the Montrachet,
aroma and flame softening
the silent corners of the room

this was his favourite time
curled together on the sheets
small flames reflected in the glasses
small moments when flesh blooms
into something more than the heaving world

ghosts are bound
by links they cannot relinquish
is it she who cannot let him go
or he who does not wish to leave
she does not care

when he is so close
that she can feel him
the outline of limbs and fingers
shimmering in the hesitant light
she raises her glass to him
her skin takes on the bloom of wine
the years fall through the air   the air
rising from her flesh he drinks
the only way he can

Clélie Rich

questionnaire

you ask what women, aging, dream of

we dream we are ripe fruit
blood oranges
we dream of pain
that halves us
ribs to groin

we dream we are filled with rich juices

these are the dreams that lie
beneath memory
that inhabit
the bones, the arteries,
the cells

we dream of a child crying
in a room whose doorway
we can never find again

Eileen Kernaghan

Like Mother

Something has inflamed my hands, and they speak
in angry blisters, little islands of rage,
each one taut with its tense pool
of ichor, and I recall my mother's hands—
an efflorescence of scarlet—
and wonder if she is railing at me
through these multiple mouths.

I have kept her bottled up, banished her
from my cadenced and careful voice,
thwarted her twitch in my gestures,
denied her in mirrors, in my anxious,
deep-set eyes. Now she has me

red-handed, she shouts
from my blotched and spotted hands,
she has lit these myriad fires,
burning eruptions that call out, 'Mother, mother.'

Ah, devious little mother, how like you
to break out in this baroque
distress signal, this mottled landscape
of complaint, declaring through my denials,
'You are like me, like me.'

Jean Mallinson

15

Forgotten Arts

I have forgotten the arts of love

I have forgotten the black arts
of love's sorcery—*ars amatoria*--
can no longer distinguish
nuances in lovers' sighs.
I have effaced, too, the white arts of mothers
their spells for growing,
charms they whisper in the night
to keep their children safe.

The domestic arts—incantations
of recipes, spreading of tables, rituals
of scrubbing—I unlearn, and turn
to the housekeeping of the world,
the sorting and recycling
of things, sweeping of water and sky.

What I have by heart, learned
at my mother's feet, to span
the infinite distance to her face,
is the arts of language—
gramarye, and *ars poetica*.
Now I summon them
to traverse the almost infinite distance
to the times and places I practised
the arts I have forgotten.

Jean Mallinson

Open stock

(for Clélie)

Our mothers wouldn't call this table 'set'.
They understand the word to mean
a regiment of matching patterns in close formation,
the shape of a sugar bowl echoed in cups
with saucers, platters and tureens serving
to reinforce the theme—florals or ancient arabesques,
solid colours with precious rims—and flatware,
released for the evening from a weighty air-tight chest.

I am better nourished
by your smorgasbord of china and a mixed bouquet
of knives and forks, each piece gathered
with abandon and panache, for love, for fun.
This Japanese rectangle, the shining Chinese bowls,
spiced with your family's British heirlooms,
somehow more convivial tonight.

On this enthusiastic table you display
fragments of appetite, a passion of variety
(subtle obverse of the usual collector's coin)
which shouts that uniformity is one
of the avoidable small deaths.

Sue Nevill

Queen of Red Clay

Some irreverent wag, looking at her
standing ... broad wooden sceptre in
her hand and her yellow turban on
her head might call her the Sultana
of Edom or the Queen of red clay ...
Elihu Burrit, 1868

She stands statuesque
her turbanned head, her thin garments
spattered with clay she works into bricks,
slaps into moulds. Her hands
lift and turn these inedible loaves.

Pale-skinned girls
blood drained by the weight of wet clay
they carry on their heads
might be her pages

if only their court was gold-painted
scented by spiced meat searing over open fires
lady and attendants dressed in silk.
Instead they smell the blaze of kilns
push each common day toward week's end
and a few pennies for the gin-palace.

Beyond the factory wall
men are building monuments to labour.
No ceremony, no queens or kings cut ribbons.
Just brick on brick, slate roofs and chimneys
stacked against a raddled sky.

Pam Galloway

juego de palmas*

these women know their purpose
clapping through the long music   everything falls
to their palms: incantations to the night
the sudden *rasgueado* of guitars
accents struck like sparks from heels

> *purpose in their*
> *palms   incantations*
> *fall like sparks from hands*

rhythm in the body
when they walk to market
feet dance patterns in the dust
when they chop meat mend clothes make love
hands are singing

> *in the dust dance patterns*
> *in the dust*
> *are singing*

some nights they clap alone
pass stories back and forth
they lean into the music
toss sparks into the night   echoes

> *night claps alone*
> *leans into the*
> *music*
> *echoes*

of guitars and voices playing
in their palms

Clélie Rich

* *chorus of clapping used in flamenco performances*

The Language of Cigarettes

The language of cigarettes is spoken
on small grey screens at one a.m.
when lovers meet, slouch-hatted,
in a chiaroscuro Berlin
or louche young men in black berets
extinguish their *Gauloises*
in *vin ordinaire.*

It is the language of another place,
another time, seductive as *langue d'oc,*
and just as fraught
with dangerous metaphor.

Eileen Kernaghan

Old Words

Power Shifts

Power shifts, maps are redrawn,
names reversed: Frobisher Bay
now Iqaluit, part of Nunavut.
The old Inuit names resurface, reclaim places
from intrusions of whalers, explorers,
missionaries, government.

The ancient names have waited
under the tundra, preserved in ice,
for the heavy pages of history to turn.
Now as the landscape
becomes a place to be at home in,
they feel good on the tongue
sounding the old syllables of what it means to be here.

Jean Mallinson

The Other Side of Life

(for the Moody Blues)

We're sitting in the park in mid-September
and all of us are fifty.
When they frisked my pack they found
two books, an extra sweater and
a thermos of hot chocolate.

A flock of geese flies overhead in close formation.
We applaud.

The Blues are fifty too. Their movements are sedate.
Behind me
a small child chatters
through "Tuesday Afternoon".

But oh, the lights, the smoke, the colours,
the bass reverberating like
a second
even more erratic
heartbeat ...

Thanks for keeping the faith, they say.
We clap, pick up our chairs
and other people's garbage.

The cops have left. They only came to hear the music.
I hum a song whose words I have forgotten
or maybe never knew.

Eileen Kernaghan

Break

I had a good home and I left
serves me jolly well right

Arms linked reef-knot tight
mother and I marched out
heels clacking in synch.
The walk from the bus to home
shortened by our song, mantra against the wind
that slapped our faces, forced our voices louder
into giggles that tripped
over our mistakes.

Stand on a nick and you'll marry a brick
and a beetle will come to your wedding

We avoided cracks between paving stones
as sure our fate lay in those lines
as when we stretched our hands open
to the fortune-teller at the fair.
We planted feet firm in adjacent squares
watched the ground, measured steps
kept within the rules
neither of us trusting slabs of concrete
that would one of these nights
break. Throw us either side of a crevasse
too wide to join hands across.

Pam Galloway

29

N.B. Make glasses in order to see moon large.

*Tell me if anything was ever done ... Was anything
ever done ... Tell me if ...*
From the last notebooks
of Leonardo da Vinci

Paintings?
A dozen or so finished. Always the light
drew me. But the world—
so full,
and time so wanting.

The sun does not move.

My water shoes, spring-driven cart,
my practical *bordello* (right-angled corridors,
three private entrances!), dissection and
the long thought of human flight ...

Heat: 50 entries. The angle of incidence ...

There was a beauty beyond paint.

... in one glance an infinity of forms:

I trusted vision; the eye does not betray us. Look
to nature, see how small we are.
The rounded waters will fall upon us, with a rush
of opposing winds and ancient trees uprooted.
The Deluge, I foresee it ...
Ah, me, how many lamentations!

Tell me, tell me if anything was ever done.

Sue Nevill

shadow of the birdfeeder

there is a woman on the shabby couch
she is reading aloud to her cat
who is asleep

> *the Buddha Gautama*
> *listed fourteen questions*
> *to which he would allow no answer*

the woman has never seen a Buddha
nor the face of any god
she does not believe
in bushes that burn and speak

> *such as*
> *is the universe*
> *infinite in space*

she hears dustballs stir under the couch
she hears her parents fighting
old words rolling through childhood
like cannons or machine gun fire
she counts greying hairs
stains on the couch
miscellaneous keys
unreturned phone calls

> *or not infinite*

the cat is confused
barely awake and unstretched
he has seen the shadow
of the birdfeeder and birds
he climbs up the woman to pounce
on the empty wall behind her

or both
or neither

his questions are not like the Buddha's
he considers sleep
and the distance between
shadows and reality

Clélie Rich

Living Ghosts

the phantom captain

after his wound had healed
the ragged edges of skin sewn
together over the knob of his knee
the peg fitted to his stump
after weeks of staring
at the brocade uniform
hanging empty
he returned to his ship

always he had felt safest on the ocean
at first perched in the crow's nest
or twined into the rigging
more recently simply swaying
in his hammock
all the motion that the sea can make
rocking him like a child

but the salt air ground itself
between his skin and the wood
the phantom toes twitched and throbbed
reminding him of nothing

the crew caught sight of him sometimes
on rare mornings when the mist rose
over the shallow seas and the moon hung
like a warning of another fatal battle

Clélie Rich

November 11th, 1994

After the rain, the Last Post, the Silence,
after the laying of wreaths, the Legion fills.
Between sobriety and bathos comes
a quiet stage of drunkenness when men
remember private wounds—lost youth,
illusion, hope—when chinks grow wide
in the high walls they hide behind, the walls
that women never learn to build.
A man turns to an old comrade, then,
and says, "I was glad to have you at my back.
You were quiet, but you were a good man ..."
"We were all good men," the other says,
and something suddenly is laid bare
that cannot be explained, or shared.

Eileen Kernaghan

In the grain

(*In memory of Bill Fairley*)

At first you watched, stood beside him
all those chilly Saturday mornings,
followed his thick yet precise hands
stroking a fine length of fir.
Timber, he called it, suggesting music
caught in the grain.

He taught you how to ease out wood's tone,
set of the saw, the start of a cut
and how to stay straight, keep time
with his steady back and forth,
his solid grip guiding your hand.

You held the tools: mortice-gauge,
set-square, bradawl and bit.
Their names, lyrics he never forgot.
You turned their weight,
tipped a spirit-level to find true.

Now, when you lean into the plane's glide
or turn a paintbrush to cut in clean,
he's there; humming the first line
over and over. Both of you
lost in the build.

Pam Galloway

step

every day they occupied
my house a trail of
footprints in the dust
little indentations in
the piles of clothes
i had to vacuum had to
pick things up i could not
sleep unless i did
everywhere they ran
ahead of me they climbed
the streaky mirrors sticky
doors oh god it was impossible
to rest the knowledge that
some sneaky feet were running
through my life the leaves
on my front walk i had to
clean i had to dust i
had to rake the yard
this
went on for months
till i collapsed got
drunk and looked around

everything
was in its place

everything
was shining

sheets pressed
shelves lined
even corners
nobody could see were
antiseptic
and in the polished
kitchen taps i saw
my mother's face

footprints
i'd been following
my mother's footprints
always in front of me
always light and when
i put my foot in one
it fit

Sue Nevill

All those years

All those years, trying
to please everyone
I was dying. To please
everyone is to be
no one, to perform
an antic masquerade.

And was my audience pleased?
My tight-lipped mother is long dead,
my ex-husband moves his lips sometimes
but his words are lost in the infinite air
between us, my children improvise
their own theatrics now, and God
has not said.

Jean Mallinson

Strings

Kandinsky's Colours

Colour is the keyboard, the eyes are the hammers,
the soul is the piano with many strings.
Wassily Kandinsky

on green days
the air shimmers like shot silk
the wind makes a small green sound
like cellos

on red days
the sun leaps through morning windows
fields ignite
the trees sing out like trumpets

on mauve days
fog clings to the hills like tattered lace
light fades from the lilac-haunted garden
the rain in the eaves makes a sad Edwardian music

on white days
time hangs suspended
the sky is the colour of a held breath
the colour of the pauses between notes

Eileen Kernaghan

long term

her first memory
is a blue tapestry
sensation of rug
presence of blue
nothing more

first grade teacher
twelfth birthday
names of lovers
all slipped by her
into some deep place
she barely touches

and when she tries
it is like finishing
someone else's weaving
picking up the coloured threads
of one classmate two more seven more
until all are continued in the pattern
she ties them into place
knots the end for safety

she is almost looking forward
to being old   she is sure
it will come back
this life whose moments she is forgetting
as quickly as she lives them
she is sure it will be there
waiting for her
something blue and familiar
in its outstretched arms

Clélie Rich

Spinning tops, chalk and string

Large hand upon a small shoulder
heads tilt together, listen

> *when I was a lad we'd spin our tops*
> *see, wind the string just tight enough*
> *then pull, just right enough. It'll go for minutes.*

Grandad teaches magic tricks:
a chalk cross spirited through wood
and facial contortions even the changing wind will fear.

> *circle the string round your hands*
> *now, thread fingers through like this*
> *and this, now PULL.*

The puzzle breaks, the cradle lost

> *there it goes now move those fingers*
> *fast lad, ready, catch it ...*

String hangs loose in hands
trained on electronic wizardry.
Grandad waits.
The boy pockets the string.
The cat falls and falls.

Pam Galloway

Labyrinth

Image of quest, of risk: the girl outside
holding the clew—the coiled ball of thread—
the man treading the maze of corridors,
lightless, smelling of old blood.
Now and then he tugs at the yarn
to make sure she is still there
at the entrance to the labyrinth.

Trust is to walk into the dark spirals
grasping a string unwinding from the hand
of a girl he scarcely knows.
As long as the thread is taut
he inches forward, knowing he can return.

Monster slain, he winds himself back
into her hands. In the end
he will abandon her, unable to bear
waking at night and knowing
he owes his fame to a slip of a girl,
a spool of thread.

Jean Mallinson

moon marks

turn in the night to face the window

you have not dreamt the light

this is the mark the moon
full and burning
makes on your sheets

mad moon

searing ice
into the brains of those
who sleep bareheaded

turn

women have died for skin this pale
and men have killed for it
strings of grave light
pulling them down

bowstrings of light
singing

> *i am the history of witches*
> *the first excuse*
> *for dance*
>
> *open the window*
> *it is large enough*
> *to climb through*
> *kiss my ivory fingernail and swear*
> *you have forgotten gravity*

drape yourself in my shocked silence
deaf to everything except
the quiet collisions
of owls
of hearts

mad moon

freezing the slow maples

open

the window

Sue Nevill

In the Thick

rough terrain

coming down
    from high places
     the ground

       falls away

there is no sure footing
        anywhere

    words
    catch at our feet
    like broken branches

      thoughts seek us out
      like the hidden eyes of animals

go carefully
    where the marsh creeps across the pathway

Eileen Kernaghan

past the bone

she is learning to remove her body
she knows she will dance better without it
without its sudden painful failures
its longing for rest   for something soft to live on

it is slow work
one step at a time
one moment at a step
the layers of skin   of flesh shedding

already she is past soft tissue
and the footwork has grown easier
movement more supple
soon she will begin on the bone
she anticipates years on the spine alone
but it could be quicker than she thinks
perhaps the dancing can carry her
through hard matter

and when she is past the bone
slow dancing through the heart and lungs
movement will be like nothing she has ever dreamed
like the air itself
in motion

Clélie Rich

The Jewish Bride

"...the light seems to come from within the figures,
almost supernaturally illuminating
their faces and garments."
          The World of Rembrandt

The light
is buried in this thick paint.
He digs for it
with palette knife his fingers
the handles of brushes
turning the surface
and turning it again.
It is a golden light
not the clear cloud-shifted mirrors
of Holland not the spare glitter
of Protestant rooms
but older
emerging slowly from a climate
leisurely with
long memories of heat.
He digs.
He turns.
The arm within the sleeve
glows the sleeve smolders canvas
ignites.

Sue Nevill

touching the past

she leans into the weight of the table
stretches her hands across the grain
lets her fingers slip into knots and cuts
stroking gently circling
scars in skin

wood breathes in her mother's silenced kitchen
she imagines scent of pine
fresh baked bread

mother always made bread
after the fights
after she'd picked herself up
splashed water on her swollen eyes
her bruised cheek

she never spoke
her mouth a straight hard line
as she cleared the table wiped away the spills
the tears   and set out flour sugar milk
weighed and measured and arranged
in precise order
she boiled water in the kettle
left it to cool
ready to bring the yeast slowly to life

she slammed the dough against the table
slapped and punched   flat hands and fists
against a smooth pale skin

they leave an impression

Pam Galloway

Through Thick and Thin

She thickens batter with flour,
thins it with milk, boils jelly
till it sheets on the lip of a wooden spoon,
rolls flaky pastry to the brink
of breaking, thickens fruit pie with tapioca,
gravy with cornstarch, simmers and stirs sauce
with a whisk till its whirlpool slows
and lingers, beats fudge till it forms
a ball in a bowl of water,
agitates slobbery egg whites into peaks,
whips viscous cream into hummocks,
heats hardened honey,
till it pours in a liquid stream.

Mistress of transformations
she watches, stirs, waits, knowing
cooking, like life, is a matter
of judging densities.

Jean Mallinson

Going to Extremes

parosmia*

his wife
cries over onions but cannot smell them
he always has to buy her perfume
chooses how he wants her to smell

sometimes at the perfume counter
his own nose plays tricks on him
and he smells blood from an open wound
something rotting in the sun
or burning yes the smell
of something burning, a woman perhaps, her hair on fire
flames licking at her skin
a woman burning as she screams at him
to stop

Clélie Rich

* *olfactory hallucination*

Blood lines

She could not quite remember how
she had slid into sorrow
the full desk the unobstructed window traded
for a husband with a false blue family line
needled into him from birth
a husband heavy with names
who miscalled her

> If I had a daughter
> (she dreamed at this time under the skin of words)
> I'd name her Shakti
> so she could shout most loudly in the darkness
> I'd call her Kali
> and watch her eat men's names and their deaf bones
> and unimportant blood
>
> Or refuse to name her
> letting her grow undefined
> until she heard her proper name
> echo off the curved walls of the world
> and recognized it

The children came   both boys
just what his longtongued mother
had produced   the only sex acceptable
to his sharp-lipped father
At the christening font revenge occurred to her
She drowned their odd old forenames till the ink dissolved
and the water ran red

Sue Nevill

Howling

3 a.m. Again. You wake.
Is it the chill in your small bones,
or is it the moon?

Moon that presses silver at the edges of curtains,
pierces through to tantalize your rhythms
pull you into cycles out of your control.

I know what the moon can do and you will learn.
You sleep again while I attend its insistent silence.
I throw back the curtains. Howl.

Pam Galloway

Female Complaint

You are an unwelcome visitor in your own house.
The chairs conspire against you.
The table squats in your path
like a brown toad.
The bed snarls and bunches itself into stiff hummocks.
Windows shutter themselves.
Keys turn in locks.

You are an unwelcome stranger in your own skin,
a handful of bones turning in a dry wind.
Blood hisses and spits,
hair crackles like torn
cellophane as you spin and spin.

You are an unwilling traveller
in your own head.
You dream incessantly of round containers
and the colour red.

Eileen Kernaghan

If Only

If only I had a name like Born-With-a-Tooth.
If only I, too, could enjoy a remarkable Indian summer.
If only my diary could replace my life.
If only my diary were not replacing my life.
If only I lived between the lines of a pastoral poem.
If only I lived between the lines of any poem.
If only I could pull myself up by my bootstraps.
If only I had bootstraps.
If only I could understand the deep structure of my computer,
    of myself, my children.
If only I could remember the meaning of 'strange attractor.'
If only most of the men I love were not dead white males.
If only God were watching me.
If only God were not watching me.
If only I could remember Indo-European roots.
If only postmodernism would go away.
If only modernism would go away.
If only ism would go away.
If only I had written, *La chaire est triste, hélas, et j'ai lu*
    tous les livres.
If only an angel would appear to me as one did to Caedmon
    and command, 'Sing me something.'
If only I knew how Sir Thomas More really pronounced 'custard.'
If only I could be mad and eloquent like Kit Smart—but then
    I'd be put away, as he was.
If only I could write "'Heighho', yawned one day King Francis"
    and not be thought precious and archaic.
If only there were some way to end an open-ended poem.

Jean Mallinson

Postcards

News From ....

Postcards from other people's lives
tell of amorous delights, despairs,
erotic trysts, adventures, escapades,
and bear stamps from far-off places
I have never seen and shall never
get to, praise exotic foods
I shall never taste.

But Kafka says
if you are attentive
in your solitary room
the dragon of reality will appear
and coil, docile, at your feet.

Waiting, I read tales
about fools who look far and wide
for treasure and in the end
find it under their own hearth stones.

Jean Mallinson

laughing down the avenues

Paris he says
and she is sixteen again
learning more French
than her mother ever dreamed of
sleeping under bridges
with baguettes chocolate and
so much wine
all that summer walking
through the Luxembourg gardens
for a morning class
along Boul St Miche
down the avenues
laughing for free

Paris he says again
and she is forty-three
she looks at his face
at how hard he works
how little they save
she tries to imagine him
sleeping on summer stone
walking cobblestones
for a cheap steak
cooked in a language
he does not understand

Clélie Rich

Ice Songs

Prayer flags dance in a white dawn.
The wind's horses leave no track upon the snow.

The voice of the flute
is the sound of a white bird singing.

Night music: beating of white wings
over frozen water.

Under the ice, moon-bubbles rise.
The fish are dreaming.

Eileen Kernaghan

always toward mountains

(for Alex)

I am looking for your landscape
through Earl Grey Southey Sareth
the roads straightforward the heights
of the horizon subtle through Dafoe
through Leroy the elevators quiet the rivers
not making a fuss and all small graves
defended by silence

the hills are rolling even-tempered
with the odd dip down to flat water

and just as I reach you
you bend the road west
your round face pulling me past Humboldt
Bruno Biggar westward
through the unambiguous sky always
always toward mountains

Sue Nevill

Parallel lines

You will see this country before me.
I flew to its furthest coast, settled
behind a wall of mountains, looked out
across islands that point west, my back to you
and the continent between us.

I have imagined Ontario, the land unfolding,
hills in the distance, maple forests
turning the horizon red. And the prairies:
one immense golden belly sunning itself
under a huge sky.

Not intimidated by its girth, you have decided
to journey across Canada's stretched skin,
your questions of geography and history
only dimples in the surface.

I will see it when I'm ready to turn
and when I'm ready to leave this rocky shelf,
the home I've stolen from the forest,
walls of hemlock, cedar, spruce, windows of rain.

I imagine you leaning from the train window
looking far into the distance
where the rail tracks converge, looking forward
to the end of your journey, where we will come together.
You are thinking about parallel lines.
How they create an illusion.
How they hold each other apart.

Pam Galloway

Unexpected   Gardens

sage hills

hours since they set out through sage
and bunchgrass windflowers hidden
roses the sweet morning wind
attentive to their sweat
over one rolling ridge
and down into the sheltered
cup before the next and up
the shallow slope clothing stitched
and itching with the sharp seeds of
late summer and at the crest
a view
of another ridge
also grassy also rolling
but higher slightly higher
with a prospect of cooler wind
and completion

they could turn again
once they were sure the horizon
had nothing left to keep from them
once they could say with certainty
we climbed we saw we know
then what pleasure
to turn again
ankles flayed for a story
a story that would bear repeating
we walked a long time they could say
but the view was worth it

the next ridge rolls
toward them
bunchgrass clutches
their shins the robber wind
of afternoon sucks at their sweat
they may fall like stones through the
thick sage air with everything still
as hidden as the roses

Sue Nevill

the roses in the carpet

she dreams she is a house
  small but spacious
when she turns over in her sleep
  another room unfolds
she is used to this
  how things can change

she dreams she is a carpet
  the roses in the carpet
  the petals of the roses
  the pollen for two bees
  who have drifted in from somewhere else

in all her rooms
there are people who know her
understand the house
and its unfolding
  rose by sudden rose

Clélie Rich

Unexpected Gardens

(in memory of Daniel)

Years since these stripped trees crashed on this beach.
They lie eased into rocks, water and wind softened,
their bark cracked, rotted into unexpected gardens.
Grass and bramble thrive in knot-holes of decay.

Plants do this. Fireweed bursts from scorched ground
and full-grown trees are rooted in sheer rock.
In the midst of death: life, pushing
slight but persistent shoots toward light.

Pam Galloway

fractal image

complex flowering
of order out of chaos—
these unexpected gardens

your disappointment:
"I thought it was a picture
of something real."

Eileen Kernaghan

A Dispraise of Mushrooms

To think too deeply about mushrooms
might be to refuse to eat them. They proliferate
in moist, dark places—caves, cellars, abandoned
coal mines, on leaf mould, moss, rotting wood—
things far gone in entropy. The little button we eat
is just the visible fruit:
the vegetable portion, underground,
is enormous, amorphous, can cover acres.
Mushrooms are a metaphor for duplicity.

And they grow so fast, spring up in a night
and are suddenly there—a stunted forest of dank surprises,
a perversion of mushrooms: fungus
is not a pretty word.

Mushrooms are obscurely sexual: the cervical cap
could have been called a mushroom. They are profligate
of spores, multitudinous: sex without blood, pallid and
pleasureless.

They will never be
an endangered species.
Like cockroaches, they will outlast us, feeding
on whatever we leave behind.

Spore prints, made
by leaving mushrooms, gills down,
on a piece of paper overnight
form dark, spoked wheels.

The prettier the mushroom, the deadlier.
They give beauty a bad name.

Barely worth eating, they are mostly water.
Dried, they turn baroque, resembling aphrodisiac roots,
desiccated, inedible-looking.
Still I buy and sauté these dubious caps
with their questionable habitat, their pleated gills,
their oblique taste.

Jean Mallinson

Secret Animals

Topiary, the whimsy of more decorated eras,
cannot be recommended here. Striking
as its animal shapes can be, the trees resent it
and, beneath their bark, grow dark and twisted,
with unfortunate effects on other plants.
Even the hardiest ancient stock will cower
from a looming gryphon, and our more pampered
modern hybrids shrink from lions.

The thick shade cast by fear will blight
your garden. It is a dreadful thing to see
a flower faint.

Sue Nevill

Butterflies

(for Rosa)

The rain is peeking out

you tell me as morning stirs
grey behind the screen of trees
outside your window.
You leave me and move on.

Look, it's a magic potato

Transfixed at the doorway
you stare at a crumb on your finger,
eat it.

Words escape from you like butterflies,
flash their brilliant reds and yellows,
sun on their wings,
rising on an updraft.
No fear of flying the wrong way
or landing on an unappreciative flower.
The garden is wide, your butterfly poems so brief.
Their startling shapes press deep into my eyes.

Pam Galloway

through the window of the garden shed

a sand bucket
left outside all summer
its bright paint chipped and peeled
into nightmare patterns
only I can recognize

a doll with no eyes
her face pierced by black holes
emptying into nothing

a heap of rags in which
one day, horribly,
something moved

this is the window I must edge past
eyes sealed shut
not daring to look through dusty panes
into corners where unspeakable
things crouch

whispering behind the glass
turn your head
open your eyes

did you think
this time
we would not be here?

Eileen Kernaghan

tonight is an angry wind

tonight is an angry wind
it passes through buildings
as if glass were panes of grass
it claws at the walls
sneers at cats and goldfish inside
a world inside a world

it is the wind of animals   summoned
from their hidden places the deer
stream along Georgia Street
push against pedestrians

moving relentlessly
across the viaducts
they stare down oncoming drivers

and after them
the ones who are unsafe
cougar bear coyote
and the sudden stealthy wolf

Clélie Rich

Breath begins

Breath begins in lungs' depths
but reaches the body's edges
to be turned into song
by vocal chords,
or music in a stopped tube.

The sequestered heart can be cardiogrammed
from its cave under the ribcage
but it cannot escape into the world
like the profligate breath,
which mingles and sings.

And what does the breath sing
while the kerneled, hermetic heart
throbs in the bloody dark?
It sings of the heart, that chambered metaphor,
and the hidden heart is content.

Jean Mallinson

At the Level of Water

lunary

the man with silvered hair
woos the moon with music
at night he lifts his face to hers
lays down a drone against which
she may or may not sing

he woos with flowers
one year he plants lunary
its pendulous discs rising
on long pallid stems
the next year he adds
starwort crescent root
and the slow phase-lily

his garden shines
with pale and singing flowers
moths and small animals gather
their large eyes full of light

he has moved so far into the night
his senses are transposed
he no longer cares to look at brightness

as flowers do he turns
blindheaded to the moon
he hears the way moths hear
the clear sigh of darkness
the soft lapping of water somewhere
the beating of a quartered heart

Clélie Rich

Flux

It is late. The end of summer.
At the level of water
she studies stilled life.
Two dragon-flies, lapis lazuli ornaments,
hang on a thread, hover
too close to the surface.
She thinks she hears the small shift,
water in flux, that is the promise of fish.
She waits for the break.

Pam Galloway

Water is verbs

Water is verbs:
ripple, flow, fall.
But immobilized in ice
it turns noun—
icicle, floe, berg—
in it trapped sounds and memories
of cascading river, swirling whirlpool,
rapids tumbling over rocks—
perpetual motion immured
in crystal stillness.

And we, too, made of water,
are verbs in our flowing, living,
liquid in our bleeding, crying,
until death nouns us and the verbs
that make us antic and kinetic
are stilled.

Jean Mallinson

Transitive

When a river is wide enough and empty it is impossible
to gauge its speed   the surface smooth as an otter's coat
the only turmoil where its edges brush the banks the way
the hem of a woman's evening gown can stir the dust in men.
Stately: ponderous and even gentle: a very slow verb: this
is the bearing of a thoroughly wide river travelling light.

And you who would not count on a woman's calm skin
a man's broad back for one split-second of security or truth
lay your body in perfect faith upon this water you never
met before and trust it will not move you. Forgetting

that rivers run inexorably to oceans and the verb is apt.

Sue Nevill

my being rises, goes to my nature*

at the level of stone
no space
no air
neither light
nor shadow   no escape
from the crushing inert weight
of collapsed stars

at the level of fire
skin, flesh, brain ignite
body becomes furnace
becomes sun
becomes incandescent
cells explode   like stars
like the sudden shattering of crystal

at the level of water
bones dissolve
into a white shimmer
of phosphorescence
on the sea's still surface

at the level of air
luminous wings lifting
lifting   into immense blue

Eileen Kernaghan

* *From a Finnish shamanist incantation*

Thoughts of the Sky

Ascension

Trees are hierarchical, hieratic.
Their trunks join under-earth with air,

their branches hold the sky up. We learn prayer
from the sound of wind in oakleaves.

In southern palms a spider weaves
the frail rope on which the soul ascends

to heaven. In arctic wind the white birch bends
its limbs to make a ladder to the clouds.

In groves of stone we gather to dispatch our gods
on skyward journeys, crowned with thorn.

Forty-three times was the Buddha born
as the spirit of a tree.

Eileen Kernaghan

cante

the man who is teaching me
to sing pours long words
into the air and waits
to weave the notes

I am learning silence
how to breathe it in
how it shifts and hums
into the bone of voice

his house has no roof
he can hear everything
his house has no walls
this is the way to listening

I am learning sound
how to hold it in the throat
and sift it
set it   lift it   let it go

Clélie Rich

Running for Paradise

As I came over Windy Gap
They threw a halfpenny into my cap,
For I am running to Paradise ...
W.B. Yeats

Even the beggar
knows that Paradise begins with
feet on the ground, one foot
after the other, the toes
bending to immovable stone,
heels digging in at first,
later to rise to a scud
of the body's making,
the ball planting, pushing,
springing to meet the strong breath
of the earth, faster
as it blows faster,
until the feet have left themselves behind
and the running is Paradise,
weightless of hours and
the chain of days,
in the wind, the heaven
of the fine free wind.

Sue Nevill

Attributes of Angels

I love the indifference of angels:
their being does not depend
on my ability to perceive them.
They do not require faith, will not grow
pale and wan because of my failure
to glimpse them.

And I love their certainty. In them,
there is no difference
between duty and desire.
Ordained in their order, unlike us,
they never long to be any closer to God
than they are.

Jean Mallinson

November Lights

Black and white dishes stack high
in a cold sink.

Walls loom grey
though I thought they were blue.

I slice vegetables. Mushrooms
pale into a shade of bone.
I can live without colour,
pare a sliver of onion, banish a tear.

November drips down the window,
the image blurs, becomes a fifties t.v.
out of tune. No theme song plays
as you arrive in the truck
move into focus.

Hero in my kitchen, you proffer fire-flowers.
You must have scorched your hand
when you reached into the sun
for these dimpled circles of light.
Yellow, yellow. They bloom against sky-blue walls.

Pam Galloway

The Other Side of Passion

The artist's wife

Wake to an empty space beside you
sheets undisturbed, after the nights he spends
with another love, unable to leave
the sensuous lines on a smooth canvas skin.

Languish in the sharp-edged smell of turpentine
linseed oil or damar varnish.
It hangs in the air for days
through all attempts to let it out,
windows and doors thrown open; or to smother it
with the scents of coffee brewing, muffins baking,
armfuls of roses carried into every room.

It's a life of lies
as he tricks your eyes into believing
three dimensions project from every flat surface.
He entices you along forest paths
to the edge of cliffs and up into the vaulted ceilings
of cathedrals. You believe him.
Then it's gone with one sweep of his brush.

He brings these certain inconveniences
but your eyes grow accustomed to noticing the sky
washed with the subtlest violet hue,
the monotone of a rock-face splintered
into yellows, blues and greens

and when he does lie beside you he talks to you
through the screen of night,
paints the fabric that is your life.

Pam Galloway

In the garden of the sixth empress

On warm days I sit by the pool in my walled garden.
Heart-shaped for remembrance,
its shallow waters are as green as celadon.
Seven tall jade trees surround it.
Hibiscus grows to the water's edge.
Where lilies trail their dark
filigree of hair,
the glittering fishes dart
through spangled light.

Moon-white against the glazed mosaic tiles
that line my pool, your luminous bones
are ivory-smooth, imperishable as alabaster.
Even now my pretty fish, my fearsome pets,
with undiminished greed pursue the shadows
of sweet flesh these lips, these gnarled
and aching fingers, once caressed.

Eileen Kernaghan

one floor below

a young man pours his guts
into his cordless phone an open window
and neighbourhood sleep

love you he cries
and lights snap on in every building

love his voice rising
over ambient curses *please!*

cats young men
in love and open windows   the trick
is to remember faintly
enough to sympathize
not enough to wake

Sue Nevill

Seeing

The last time I saw him, his bag of tricks
had not changed: predictable, stale jokes,
the clown's frantic grimace, the hollow man's
falsetto, antics of a pantaloon.
I would not have been amazed
to see him balance a glass of wine
on his bulbed nose or crawl on his knees
and bark like dog or seal.
He even had the nerve to speak to me
as though he were someone real.

I say I saw him, but what did I see?
A smiling social man whom I no longer love:
his aura shrunk, his mask
askew: a bare, forked man,
defrocked emperor. We should be
invisible except to the eyes
of love. When love's optics fail
it is not bearable to be seen at all.

Jean Mallinson

affidavit

I make oath and say that I am the petitioner

so much work
to reach this place
to make oath and say I am

*that there is no possibility of reconciliation between me
and the respondent spouse*

and where would we find words
the small tongue of my poems
carets and brackets of your software
these are two different translations

*that I verily believe that the facts alleged
in the petition for divorce are true*

I have never believed in facts
thin and unrevealing
they do not love us
only in the moments between facts
do we see another person

*that the photograph is a true likeness
of the respondent spouse*

your mirror face used to shock me
angles distorted
eyes unequal and tilted
looking at me looking
at you   which face is true
likeness

*that the certificate of marriage fully and correctly
describes the true particulars of my marriage
to the respondent spouse*

look closer
those were only the formal names
we wore to match our sweet new clothes

between the lines
smaller names were dressing themselves
learning to lift their heads

make oath and say I am

Clélie Rich

Broken Syllables

Breakdown

Slow taps dedicate
metal to mirror.
A hammer is learning its life

knows the moment
the whole will give up
its tenuous grasp on perfection

break into syllables
fractured soliloquies
words that slide

like raindrops down a window-pane.
A small pool without shape
soon evaporates

leaves a dead-calm
surface. Reflection
ready to fragment.

Pam Galloway

the weight of breathing

she always spoke from smoke
pausing only to inhale
so that Portuguese sounded hesitant
Russian thicker
the syllables of each
new language slurred
by the weight of breathing

language was her life
and when she died
her doctors found nests
of grammar growing in her
    Latin at the base of the spine
    the whole of Europe spreading
    towards her mouth and hands

Clélie Rich

plain chant

> *When you have a psalter you will wish to have a breviary, and when you have a breviary you will sit in a chair like a great prelate and say to your brother, 'Brother, bring me my breviary.'*
>
> Francis of Assisi

out of the darkness, a voice
singing of birds and the flavour
of plain water, the luxury of sun
on a bare wall

look at this thin human hand:
light, and already rising up to heaven
love this tree, this man, this horse
and carry a weightless scrip

in comfortable cells his brothers
consider their broidered cushions
bolts slam on monastery doors

and the people hear
small daily words, understandable
and warm, recognize
the centuries they've waited
for weighty syllables to break down
into love

Sue Nevill

Speech Acts

The gods speak in light, in a burning bush,
in a shower of gold.
But we mortals turn air
into syllables: in the beginning
ba, ma, la—the babble
that will become words.

And later, in love or grief,
words shatter again into syllables,
fragmented by sobbing,
gasping for breath.

Dying, will I whisper a complete word,
one of the primal syllables—*ba, ma, la*—
or some new sound, beyond phonemes,
vowels, consonants, as I edge towards
the speechless gods?

Jean Mallinson

broken syllables

fifty centuries of sun and blowing sand
and what remains are love songs
hymns and elegies
lists of long-dead kings
and bills of lading

lines, phrases, syllables fragmented
by uncertainties and errors
mysterious lacunae

in Sumerian, love is a compound verb
it means "to measure the earth"

I built my (house), a shrine, in a pure place,
I called it with a good name ...
its shade stre(tches) over the snake-marsh,
the lofty marshland stretches out its arms to me
bends (?) its neck to me.
Sing sweet songs, cause the river to rejoice ...

the eye is the hieroglyphic for "to see"
"to weep" is the eye with a fringe of tears

Your daughters have ... for you in their (?) ...
Your ... sweet sounds ... sleep
The ... lament for you (?) does not cease

joy, honour, courage,
grief, ambition
these hard imperishable nouns
are scoured into stark relief
by wind and water and the slow abrasion of the years

(The Tigr)is is surre(ndered) to him, as (to a rampant bull).
The churn lies (shattered).
The cup lies (shattered). Dumuzi lives no more,
the sheepfold is given over to the wind ...

[Remaining nineteen lines destroyed]

Eileen Kernaghan